THE 7 JUSTIFIED SLAYERS

"I'm Good Where I Am Because..."

Tammie T. Polk

Cover designed by Author
Photo by Aron Visuals on Unsplash

Tammie T. Polk
Visit my website at www.tammieterrellmompreneurs.com/bookstore

Printed in the United States of America

First Printing: March 2020
Amazon/KDP

ISBN-13 9798630960030

This book is dedicated to the woman who feels that she can't achieve her goals because of the demands placed on her life already...

CONTENTS

WAIT...THESE SEEM FAMILIAR!

Yes, you've seen them before...

If you've read my book, "Warrior Women: Overcoming the Slayers God's Way," you'll see that these were listed at the very end of the book. I chose to give them their own space because they have become so prevalent!

At a time when the phrase "Mom Guilt" has become a personal mantra for many women, it's time to squash that! As a mom who ears many hats, you must understand that your dreams matter and you don't have to sacrifice every single thing in your life...

If I say anything more, I will steal the thunder of my chapters...

I'M NOT THERE/READY YET!

You can STILL start...

Let me start rather bluntly and ask why you think you aren't ready? If I were to take a guess, I would say that you are looking at someone else online or even in person who has you thinking that what you have or are trying to build isn't good enough.

When people ask you what you're waiting on, how many times do you say things like this:

"I've got to wait until my ___________ finishes ___________."

"I've got to get my _______________ first before I do that."

"I've got to help my ___________ get their___________ going first."

"I need to have ____________ before I can get started."

Regardless as to which one of these you've said, it's time for you to get out there and let people know something about you, your mission, and your message. What is it that you think you're missing that's so important that you can't even tell people that it's coming up or out soon?

Let's revisit the quotes from the previous paragraph. We're going to talk about the first one in the next chapter, so we will focus on the others.

First, do you think that you need a degree or certification before you get started? That's not the case! Many entrepreneurs start their businesses long before they get a degree. Many of the most successful CEOs didn't get them until later in life and some never got them at all!

Yes, we live in a world where people want to see these things; however, there are so many things that you can still do in the meantime. For example, you don't need a degree or certification to:

- Name your business
- Create a logo and branding for your business
- Decide who your target market will be
- Decide what products and services you want to offer and at what price
- Start social media pages for what you want to do and garner interest
- Network and get ideas
- Write a business plan

You may need HELP doing those things, but they can still be done while you continue your education. There is a plethora of people out there who can help you with this because they, too, took the same road.

I think about my business coach, Tameka, who only had an associate's degree when she started her business. She didn't let that stand in her way and she has become one of the world's most sought after parenting and confidence experts.

I think about my Dad, who has worked in the same industry for over 40 years with an associate's degree in electrical engineering.

I think of myself, who taught in the classroom from the age of 12 with a degree in psychology. Despite that, I was recognized as one of the most requested substitute teachers in two school districts.

Also, understand that there are different ways to educate yourself! Joining someone's Facebook group or coaching program can give you many of the tools that you are going to school for! One of the BEST branding and marketing classes that I've ever taken was conducted by a fellow homeschool mom...think about it!

Are there entrepreneurs going back to school? Yes, and they have their reasons; however, they didn't allow those reasons to keep them from getting started and neither should you.

Second, if you're waiting to get your life together before you get started, then you will never get anything done. As I read in a recent article, the chicken crossing the road didn't wait until the conditions were perfect, he simply crossed the road!

"Imperfect action is better than no action" was a quote that I heard from a doctor I recently interviewed for my online summit. That quote spoke volumes to me because it reminded me of how much time we spend trying to make something perfect before we put it out. The problem with that is that you will ALWAYS find something wrong if you go looking for it...

I will never forget when a client of mine refused to publish her book because she didn't receive one person's endorsement. She didn't feel like what she had was good enough to go out unless she had that one person's endorsement.

I tried to encourage her to go ahead with the two endorsements she already had, and she simply wouldn't budge. Finally, she found another excuse to use, which was money... I debunked that one, too, because she thought that she needed $500 to make her book what she wanted it to be and I'd helped her find quality services for less than that—the book STILL isn't out!

Whatever you're waiting on isn't worth the health of your entire vision, Sweetheart! I recently had a conversation with a pastor, and we talked about how so many in life, business, and ministry are DYING with life-altering knowledge that can change LIVES! With the rapid decline of people scrolling through social media, one of the best places you can put your knowledge is on the BLANK PAGE!

Think about an immediate need that what you are holding on to will solve. The problem is that you think that you need something else to solve that problem and you DON'T! Then, when someone tells you that, you dismiss it and tell them what you're trying to get going when what you need is sitting right in front of you collecting dust and cobwebs.

I remember when life hit like that for me. My first book had just come out and we were in dire straits. Our bills were paid, but that was it. We had nothing left with two weeks before either of us got paid again. I knew that my book would keep my family going and we found the money to make the first order.

Long story short, I tripled what we spent on that shipment of books. With every sale, I bought something for the house or put gas in the car. With that $12 in my hand, I looked around my house for a need that would be met with that very $12. Once I found a need, I took care of it.

What are you REALLY waiting for?

Third, putting others before yourself has its place; however, when you are CLEARLY sacrificing you, your mission, and your message for theirs, that's a PROBLEM. And, it's a big problem if the person you're helping is trying to stop you from helping them so that you will focus on what YOU are supposed to be doing.

Disney's "The Rookie" is one of my favorite movies. When the players on the high school baseball team saw their coach's talent, they made him a deal. If they made it to the state championship, he had to go to a major league tryout. When they made it to state, each one of those young men looked him in the eye and said, "It's your turn, Coach." He went to the tryout, made the team, and the entire town turned out to see him play when he came back home! Let that sit for a minute.

Here he was trying to help them to become better young men as well as ballplayers, but he had a goal of his own that he was sitting to the side for their sakes. They weren't having it! Pay attention if you have someone like that around you because everyone isn't a leech or a mooch. There ARE people out there who want to see you do what YOU are meant to do and serve those YOU are meant to serve.

Don't get mad and say that you have time...we're going to talk about that later.

Lastly, do NOT allow Shiny Object Syndrome to keep you from getting started! YOU DO NOT HAVE TO HAVE EVERYTHING THE INFLUENCERS YOU FOLLOW HAVE! You will be surprised at how simple some of their processes are, but the way it's presented makes you think that they are spending THOUSANDS when they're not!

Case in point—one of my graphic designers. She recently redid her website and I thought it was BEAUTIFUL and I got jealous very quickly. I was FLOORED when she told me that she was using the very tools that I used daily to make her website what it was— YouTube, Adobe Acrobat, Google Drive, and Acuity! And which of these do I have? ALL OF THEM! I immediately started playing around with things to see if I could duplicate what she did. Why? It's because I say that it wasn't going to cost me another red copper PENNY to do it....

I want to close this chapter out with a challenge. I want you to think about this Justified Slayer and what it has truly cost you. Where could you have been had you not allowed these to sidetrack you and what are you going to do moving forward?

This doesn't have to kill you, your dreams, and your goals...not at ALL!

TIME TO SLAY THE

SLAYER...

What is it that you want to get done?

____

____

____

____

____

What are you allowing to stop you?

____

____

____

____

____

Why is that thing more important that what you want to get done?

____

____

____

____

If you put your thing first, how much different would things be for you?

____

____

____

____

Is this thing really an issue or you are simply making excuses to get people to stop asking you about it?

____

____

____

What's the plan to stop this Slayer from gaining any further ground?

I HAVE TO TAKE CARE OF MY FAMILY FIRST!

Mom's Dreams Matter, Too!

We are natural planners, yet we don't use those skills for ourselves. When you found out you were pregnant, what did you do? You started planning.

You read books...

You asked friends about doctors, baby products, and even daycares and preschools...

You started savings accounts and even 529 plans...

You laid out their nursery...

You attended every parenting class you could find...

You spent hours researching who, what, when, where, why, how, and how much...

Why? It's because you wanted to make sure that absolutely everything was ready for your little bundle of joy when they came into the world, right?

The same applies to you and the goals that you have for yourself. How so? Let's talk about it.

As parents and parental figures, we tell the children in our lives how important it is for them to read. When they struggle with it, we reach out for help. We threaten them with punishments if they don't read and make sure that any reading assigned by their teachers is done...but what about you?

Let me share some statistics with you:

- 33% of those who graduate from high school and 42% of those who graduate from college will never read another book in their lives.
- Only 43% of new books purchased are read to completion.
- Only 30% of adults living in the US have been to a bookstore in the last 5 years.
- Only 20% of families living in the US have bought or read a book in the last year

- Reading helps children to better understand the emotions of others.
- 1 hour of reading will make you an international expert in 7 years.

Which one of those statistics have you fallen prey to? Probably more than one. When I worked in the school system, Read Across America Week was one of my favorite events because it meant that the teachers were pitted against the students to see which group read the most books. The reward was a half-day of work or school for the winning group!

Do you know what this challenged us to do? No longer be a statistic! When we had our Drop Everything and Read Day, the principal checked to make sure that every ADULT was reading. It didn't matter what it was, but we had to be reading.

It is said that the most successful CEOs read 50-60 books a year...let that marinate for a second.

"So, Tammie, what does this have to do with me putting my family first?" More than you realize!

It is dangerous to prioritize a goal for someone else when you don't have that goal yourself. If you're not working toward that goal, the person in your family that you're trying to motivate won't see it as necessary for them to do. You set the tone for whatever happens in your family, so what you do every day matters!

Second, when was the last time you asked for a recommendation of a product or service that YOU needed? If we are honest, we don't do this for ourselves until either something breaks or goes wrong. Don't believe me? Scroll through your Facebook feed and see how many people are asking for recommendations for something that's a PROBLEM—even when it comes to their health!

I challenge you to focus on your needs. You're no good to anyone in your family if you're broke, despondent, busted, and disgusted...moving on!

Third, if you looked at how you have spent money for the last 7 days, would you be able to say what you spent on yourself? While in a store once, I watched a woman put some lipstick back after receiving a text from her child that they needed some supplies for a school project and that hurt me... She mumbled that it was always something and that she could never do anything for herself. Does it have to be that way?

There are times when I am out and about and will stop to treat myself to a good meal or a cheat snack, not thinking twice about it! Do I make sure that I eat it and that all evidence is gone by the time I make it home? Sure, but not always. Have I lied about how I got it? Yes, I have. Have I enjoyed mine and then both something for them? More times than I care to even think about!

My point is that you don't have to always sacrifice like that... This may sound cruel, but they don't have to have everything that you get! It doesn't always have to be that "I bought it for me, so I need to buy it for them" trap of mom guilt. As my business little sis, Christina, says, "Bump them kids! I'm special, too!"

There is nothing wrong with you doing something for you...

Even when it comes to saving, it doesn't have to be for a rainy day or their education—it could be for yours or something else that YOU want... That money doesn't even have to be kept in the same PLACE as the rest of your money! What is something that YOU want that you can save up to get?

Fourth, when it comes to buying anything new for your home, do you put the kitchen, bathroom, living room, or kids' room before your master bedroom? I need you to not do that... Yes, I love surprising my kids with new stuff, too, from time to time, but MY master bedroom is ALWAYS a part of ANY redecorating plan in my house and it's done FIRST! All other rooms are decorated in the order they are received.

I understand that you want to see them happy, I really do! However, you should walk into your room and have the EXACT same joy that they do...

When we moved into our first rental home in 2010, I remember putting our girls in their rooms at bedtime. We'd bought everyone new linens and everything! Once I put them to bed, I took a shower and then sprawled out in the middle of my bed dressed in new linens. I sighed and smiled because, for the first time, I was in my bed without any kids and sleeping on new linens! Let me tell you—NOTHING feels better than getting into a freshly dressed bed after a shower and I'm willing to argue about that!

Seriously, though...when was the last time you redid YOUR bedroom or work area?

Fifth, when was the last time you sat through training or a webinar that wasn't required by your child's school or your job? When was the last time you watched a tutorial to make something YOU were interested in?

Not only that, have you been fighting with the decision to go back to school or even continue your education? I watched my mother grapple with this. She married young, didn't finish high school, and I was 14 before she decided to finish her education. I am the youngest of my siblings, so she waited a VERY long time as my oldest brother was born in 1975 and I was born in 1981—she started in 1995. Are you and my mom twins?

I watched my mom build a business from what she learned. She was the first entrepreneur I ever saw... She loved what she did and those whom she served. Now, she still stayed on us about our education; however, I remember her asking me to leave my computer on so she could practice her typing skills. I sat in class with her and watched her presentations. I helped her take better notes. We were a TEAM! I'll let you think about that...

Finally, when was the last time you went without sleep to find something that YOU needed? We often search high and low for what our family needs, yet we will go for the first thing we can find for ourselves...

Listen, I'm in no way saying that you can't do for your family, but remember this: You yourself are your first and primary business. If you don't take care of you, then you CAN'T put them first!

TIME TO SLAY THE SLAYER...

What is it that you want to get done?

____

____

____

____

____

____

What are you allowing to stop you?

____

____

____

____

____

____

Why is that thing more important that what you want to get done?

____

____

____

____

____

If you put your thing first, how much different would things be for you?

____

____

____

____

____

Is this thing really an issue or you are simply making excuses to get people to stop asking you about it?

____

____

____

____

What's the plan to stop this Slayer from gaining any further ground?

THAT'S NOT FOR ME

Really? Or is it that you just don't

want to try?

I understand that everything presented to you may not be your cup of tea; however, you know within yourself that you have dismissed something presented to you, knowing FULL well that it is something that you NEED to do....

As I said in the previous chapter, we sometimes won't take advantage of things until something goes wrong instead of working on it and having it waiting in the wings. We will excuse away its purpose in our lives and what it will do simply because we don't want to do the work. We want everything to be easy and it won't be that way.

You won't be able to do everything on your phone...

You won't always be able to have what you need in the way or on the phone you want it to be on...

There won't always be an app for it...

You might have to post about it more than once...

You may even have to SHOW YOUR FACE ONLINE!

In times like these, we honestly can't afford to dismiss anything, especially if it's something that we KNOW that we can do, are good at, and enjoy doing. Do I turn down a lot of the opportunities presented to me? Yes, I do, if it seriously doesn't align with what I want to do at that time.

Have I ever taken advantage of an opportunity and regretted it? Yes, I have; however, I have also taken opportunities that I thought I wouldn't like and then ended up wondering why I'd never done it before that time.

Like me, you may have people in your life who try to push you to do certain things because they can see that you would rock at it...don't be too quick to hit them with "That's not for me" and I'll tell you why...

I once met a woman who had a wealth of knowledge. She had a word for everybody, no matter what the situation was. After she would say something profound, she would sit and journal about the whole encounter. One day, she allowed me to read it and I told her that it would make a great book.

"Naw...that author stuff ain't for me," she said, completely dismissing my idea. Word about her got around and she started being asked to share more about her experiences with people. Person after person said the exact same words I said to her and they received the exact same response.

A short time after this, she lost her job. She qualified for severance pay, yet it was going to run out fast. So, what did she do? She started reaching out to all those people who had presented different opportunities to her. The problem was that some were no longer available, pricier, and required more of a commitment than before. This made her angry and so much so that she accused people of lying and price gouging her...that wasn't the case.

She finally gets to me and I give her the same spill from when we'd talked before. She said that there had to be something else that she could do, and I wished her well in finding whatever she thought that would be.

She called me back when she was one month away from being completely broke. A publisher friend of mine was running a special on book creation and I told her that, if she was serious, I would help her with paying for it. She hesitated and then said she'd call me back. I told her that she had until the special ended to get back to me. She did come back...an HOUR before the special closed.

Fast forward...the people who were inviting her to share her story found out about the book and she secured a five-figure speaking engagement JUST as her severance money ran out...

While authorship may not be your thing, there is something that has been presented to you that you need to stop shirking. What you are sitting on could be the one thing that changes the trajectory of your life. You've heard me say this before, but what's in you is meant to save or to change someone's life, faith, family, ministry and/or business so how DARE you keep it to yourself?!

No matter what kind of opportunity you are presented, listen, look at all the facts and nuances, pray about it, and come back with an INFORMED decision...not one made from haste. Many of us are creating our own lean times because of "that's not for me."

What has been presented to you that you said no on without thinking? Was it something that you need to go back and reconsider?

If it's not illegal, immoral, life-threatening, or takes you away from God or your family too much, it's worth looking into...

TIME TO SLAY THE

SLAYER...

What is it that you want to get done?

____

____

____

____

____

____

What are you allowing to stop you?

____

____

____

____

____

____

Why is that thing more important that what you want to get done?

____

____

____

____

____

If you put your thing first, how much different would things be for you?

____

____

____

____

____

Is this thing really an issue or you are simply making excuses to get people to stop asking you about it?

____

____

____

____

____

____

What's the plan to stop this Slayer from gaining any
further ground?

____

____

____

____

____

____

I'VE GOT TIME

You Sure About That?

That's what you THINK! How many times have you looked at the date on something and said, "Oh, it lasts THAT long? I've got time." You go on about your merry way, thinking that you do have time to wait for whatever you're looking at.

That view is called object permanence—we think that people, places, and things will always be around for us right where they were. We don't think that anything's going to happen, so we become lax and complacent.

Then, the plot thickens...

You finally remember to go back to that thing and one of the following has happened:

- It has gone bad and must be tossed out.
- It has been discontinued and is no longer available. If you DO find it, it's at an

astronomical price that you wouldn't even consider paying.

- Its price has gone up dramatically.
- It has expired and you have no way to get it, meaning that you must wait until it's available again...if it ever is!

The funny thing about this is that there is always someone or something else to blame for this. We fuss at the first person that we see, talking about how unfair it is that this has happened. We won't accept the fact that time has gotten away from us and that we dropped the ball on taking advantage of that thing.

Suddenly, people are wrong for having deadlines and we think that they should make exceptions because we forgot. When that's not the case, then we drag their names through the mud, only to be reminded that there was a deadline to start with.

You frantically flock to social media or the phone and expect them to move Heaven and Earth for you because you forgot. You don't think that you should have to wait, pay a higher price, nor be placed on a waiting list. You feel as though they should fix it and give you what you want... That's not how things work.

During one of my boot camps, I encountered this very scenario. The program lasts for thirty days and then I give participants an additional seven days to catch up before everyone is removed from the group and it's cleared out for the next group.

Well, I had one participant who didn't do the work the entire thirty-seven days allotted to message me about not being able to find the group anymore. I explained to her that the thirty days were over and so was the extension. If she wanted back in, she would have to pay again, and she didn't think that she should have to do that.

She admitted that she should have taken it more seriously; however, I had provided what she'd paid for, so it wasn't on me that she didn't do the work and protect her investment. She proceeded to drag my name through the mud, even enlisting an attorney. The attorney contacted me, and I explained how I had provided everything that was promised, showing everything that I had done. This lady had no case because she had indeed opened the email, downloaded the material, joined the Facebook group, viewed all the posts, and commented on several of the posts.

She came back to me later and apologized for what she'd done; however, I was busy doing damage control. She ended up paying to work with me one on one.

What you must understand is that people had deadlines because of the preparations that they have to make based on the number of people they are expecting as well as the number of people who have confirmed their involvement for whatever it may be.

If it is a webinar, people must make sure that they have another space for everyone to be able to attend.

If it is an in-person event, people must make sure that they have enough space, materials, food, etc. For this reason, they can't make the concessions that you want them to make.

But, what about life in general? The same sentiment applies.

Your child brings you a permission slip for a field trip. You look at the date and see that it's several weeks away, so you pin it on the fridge and say that you have time. You fuss at your child for reminding you all the time, telling them how much time you think you have.

Field trip day comes, and you take your child to school, only to find out that your child is the only one not going on the trip. Since it had to be paid for ahead of time, you're begging the school to allow your child to go. Now you must find someone to keep your child for the day because it's an all-day trip and you must work. Either that or you call in to work, follow the bus to the place, pay full price, and hope that your child has just as much fun.

Or, there's an event that you want to go to that's a week out, so you put ONE reminder on your phone about it. You see posts and reminders to register and you keep saying that you're going to get to it. If someone asks if you are going, you tell them that you're going to get your ticket soon. Next thing you know, you're messaging the event organizer asking if you can pay at the door.

Or, it's something health related. Your doctor is telling you that you need to change how you care for yourself. You say that you have time before anything happens. You ignore the symptoms that start to develop and dismiss them as stress or tiredness. Soon, you're in the ER hoping that it's not whatever your doctor said it could be!

Or, it's your car. You see that warning light, yet you say that you've got time because you know your car. Then, you end up on the side of the road angry because no one is answering their phone and you're thinking about all the things you must do. You can't do anything other than wait and kick yourself because you know you should've dealt with that light when it first came on.

All these examples are to show you that you need to take ANY time you have seriously.

TIME TO SLAY THE SLAYER...

What is it that you want to get done?

____

____

____

____

____

____

What are you allowing to stop you?

____

____

____

____

____

Why is that thing more important that what you want to get done?

____

____

____

____

____

If you put your thing first, how much different would things be for you?

____

____

____

____

____

Is this thing really an issue or you are simply making excuses to get people to stop asking you about it?

____

____

____

____

What's the plan to stop this Slayer from gaining any further ground?

IT DOESN'T TAKE ALL THAT

There isn't always another way...

Let me put out a disclaimer here: There WILL be times when you will be presented with a solution to an issue that IS absolutely RIDICULOUS! Allow me to explain.

I was having an issue invoicing my clients, so I reached out to the company for the app I was using. They told me to have my clients to open the invoice from a computer using an incognito browser tab, clear their cache, and then pay. People don't want to do all of that just to pay someone! I told them that was too many steps, so I went back to using what I had before that.

On the other hand, we often dismiss things that we think take too much to obtain. We will ask someone who is successful in life and business what they did to get there. They tell us exactly what it took—no colors, no flavors, no junky stuff! Once they're finished, we dismiss everything that they said because we think that we can find another, shorter, easier way to get to where they are.

Let me tell you that won't always work! The shortcut that you want to take can end up costing you in the short and the long run. Just because it's shorter, easier, or even cheaper doesn't mean that it's going to work the same way.

Cheaper is the one that we often go to first, so let's look at that one. You will go to someone whom you know is worth every dime that they charge and try to lowball them. You will tell them about x or y who does it for a cheaper amount and then you're angry because that person won't bend. And, if they're the blunt type, they'll tell you to go and do business with them and that you'll be back when you're unsatisfied. You'll be walking around with subpar products and services because you don't want to go back to the person you should have paid.

The thing about that is they probably already know, especially if it's someone they heard negative things about in the past. They may know exactly what you're headed for and remember how they tried to warn you, but you wouldn't listen.

Now you're coming to them asking them to help you fix the problem created by you taking the cheap route. You have no choice but to do what they're asking you to do...it doesn't have to be that way! Also, don't be surprised at the increased price of said help...

Easier is the second one; however, you should know that easier is a two-edged sword. Easier isn't always better because there will be times when you will be presented with a situation so that your action and decision-making skills are tested.

The person asking you to do a task already knows about the easy way, yet they want to see how you operate, especially if it's a time-sensitive issue. It's not about you coming up with the easiest solution, it's about making tough decisions and producing under pressure.

Have you ever heard the story of the son-in-law and the wedding gift gone wrong?

A man went to his future son-in-law and told him to build a house. He said to spare no expense in building the house. Well, this son-in-law thought that he would impress his future father-in-law by saving money, so he started cutting corners, using subpar materials and contractors to build the house. When the house was finished, he had his chest stuck out as his future father-in-law complimented him on the way the house was built. That chest deflated faster than a popped balloon when he told him that he'd just built his wedding present.

He was SICK because he knew what he and his future bride would be living in a subpar house. He fell prey to cheaper and easier. Shorter is just as bad!

In some cases, not taking full advantage of the time that you've been given to complete a task can be detrimental to you and the project itself. There's nothing wrong with checking, double-checking, and triple-checking to make sure that everything is as its best.

I remember watching an episode of a cooking competition show. The contestants had forty-five minutes to make their best dish. One of the contestants made a SALAD...yes, you read that right...a salad. He stood around while everyone else was chopping, frying, baking, and slicing. When he presented his salad, the chef chided him for not taking the time seriously. He had forty-five minutes and presented a world-famous chef with a salad—and a basic one at that! All the ingredients were cold, so there was ZERO effort put into his dish.

When you don't take all the time allotted to you, there is a change that you may miss something important. Not only that, but you may also find something that worked better than what you prepared, yet you've already turned it in and don't want to look bad by submitting something else. You don't want anyone to ask why you didn't take the time to do that at first. Can you see the slippery slope that you're creating?

If you have the time, use it ALL unless you are certain without a shadow of a doubt that you DON'T need all that time. Your reputation is at stake.

TIME TO SLAY THE

SLAYER...

What is it that you want to get done?

____

____

____

____

____

____

What are you allowing to stop you?

____

____

____

____

____

Why is that thing more important that what you want to get done?

____

____

____

____

____

If you put your thing first, how much different would things be for you?

____

____

____

____

____

Is this thing really an issue or you are simply making excuses to get people to stop asking you about it?

____

____

____

____

What's the plan to stop this Slayer from gaining any further ground?

I'M NOT QUALIFIED

"You can do that because you're qualified to do that because of all of the experience you have." This is what my late aunt Phyllis said to me when I mentioned that I was homeschooling my children. To her, my education was the reason why I could teach my own children, not the fact that I was their mother and knew them better than anyone. Because of sentiments like this, many people doubt the skills that they have, and it hurts me to my core.

Who told you that you weren't qualified? More importantly, do they even KNOW? See, people will have misconceptions about you because they haven't seen all that you can do. Many times, they are judging you based on ONE instance that they saw THAT ONE time way back when. Because they hold that against you, you hold it against yourself and you need to quit doing that! Why? I'll tell you.

First, people will tell you that you're not qualified for something because whatever you're going for will cause you to leave them behind in some way. They want you to do better, yes, but not if they aren't, so they will keep you back from it.

Second, people will tell you that you're not qualified for something because whatever you're going for will cause you to make more money and have more freedom than they do. They want you to do better yes, but only if they have the same thing.

Third, people will tell you that you're not qualified for something because whatever you're going for will cause them to admit that all the trash they talked about you was invalid. They don't want you to do better because then they will have to admit that they were wrong about you.

Fourth, people will tell you that you're not qualified for something because whatever you're going for will cause them to end up working FOR or serving UNDER you in some way. Now, this one I MUST elaborate on further.

A lady who served as the director of curriculum and instruction wanted to go for a higher position in the school that she worked in. When the dean of that department found out, she started trying to talk her out of applying for the position. Why? It meant that, if this lady got it, she as the dean would have to report to someone who was currently her subordinate. So, she told her that she wasn't qualified...and the lady believed her. When the executive director of the school asked her why she didn't apply, she told him about the conversation she'd had with the dean. He laughed and said that it was a bunch of nonsense and interviewed her right then!

In this case, people don't want you to do better if they know you will have any type of authority over them. They know that you are about your business, so they don't want you anywhere around them because you will ERADICATE that comfort zone they've built around them!

"But, Tammie, what if that's not the case?" I get it...it very well could be a different case; however, I will encourage you to go for it anyway. Here's why...

A man wanted to pursue a higher position in his job but didn't because he didn't meet the educational requirements for the job. The hiring manager overheard him saying this to a colleague and decided to look over his file. The man was a high performer and had been so for the last five years—high review scores, very few complaints and even fewer disciplinary actions, and had helped others pursue higher positions.

The hiring manager then looked at those educational requirements and determined that his time on the job was the equivalent of what they were requiring from classroom study. He went and found the man and told him that if he really wanted to pursue a higher position, he would waive the educational requirements due to his track record.

Not enough to convince you? Let me make it personal. Remember me talking about being a substitute teacher? Well, there was this one time when not being a licensed teacher didn't matter when the school had a major need.

I ended up being the first person they reached out to about the need. For four months, I worked as a full-time teacher on a full-time teacher's salary...as a sub...with a degree in psychology.

It didn't matter to them that I wasn't a certified and licensed teacher; what mattered to them was that I had shown them that I could manage a classroom! The kids respected me, and the other teachers liked working with me—that mattered more than what my degree was in. Sound familiar yet?

Don't psyche yourself out because you never know what people will say. They just may change things simply because they know who you are, the level of work you do, and the attitude you have.

"Well, I don't have..." will close more doors than you will ever know. Change that to, "I may not have XYZ, but I CAN...." It just might be enough.

TIME TO SLAY THE

SLAYER...

What is it that you want to get done?

____

____

____

____

____

What are you allowing to stop you?

____

____

____

____

____

Why is that thing more important that what you want to get done?

____

____

____

____

____

If you put your thing first, how much different would things be for you?

____

____

____

____

____

Is this thing really an issue or you are simply making excuses to get people to stop asking you about it?

____

____

____

____

What's the plan to stop this Slayer from gaining any further ground?

I HAVE NO SUPPORT

Yes, you do...It just may not be

who you want it to be!

You may have heard this a million times, but your friends, family, loved ones, and church members will be the last ones to support you! Even if they do, they may do so out of obligation and not because they need or want what it is that you offer. I see this all the time in families of entertainers.

When you're in a family of go-getters, you want to be supported because you meet a need and not because they don't want anyone coming down on them for not supporting you. A singer once asked her family if they liked her album. They replied yes and that they'd gotten it. They became annoyed with her when she asked again and then asked what they liked about it. They couldn't answer her...

"Well, Tammie, I'd rather have that kind of support than what I'm going through with having none..." Think about that statement. Is all support good support? Just as all money isn't good money, all support isn't good support! I would rather have someone not support me at all than to support me with an ulterior or messed up motive.

Not having support at all and not having genuine support can hurt and are the same. Although it's easier said than done, you must keep going despite both scenarios.

Not having support or genuine support doesn't make who you are and what you're doing less valuable. Validation seeking will have you cowering in a corner somewhere scared to talk because you don't want to say anything that will drive people away. That's no way to live nor work!

Someone somewhere sometime somehow someway sometime needs that something that you do, so you must get clear on who they are, where they are, how you can serve them, and where to find them. The last letter in "No" is the first letter in opportunity.

To say that you're good where you are because you have no support means that you have given up on doing what you're meant to do and serving who you're meant to serve. Is the person that you wish would support you worth the person who is waiting to do so?

I gave up on my dream of opening a school because my mom died and couldn't be here to support me. I still have all my notes, documents, classroom diagrams— everything. But you know what? Every time I think about pursuing it, I remember that she's not here. I spent the bulk of my early entrepreneurial life taking what I'd developed with my mom and making it work for others. Because I didn't have her, I didn't think it was worth doing anymore...Now, I'm taking what I've created and COACHING others THROUGH making it work—a BIG difference!

Whether it's not there or ingenuine, you can't allow yourself to give up as I did. The second that you give up, you're going to have to face those who wouldn't support you and all their criticism. They will pacify you by saying that, if you go back to it, they will support you. While that may be true, it may not be something you can trust.

You show them who you are and what you can do by moving forward despite them! Go back to what you gave up because they wouldn't stand behind you. What you gave up is going to provide for those very people in some way...just wait and see. I've seen it happen myself as I have paid bills, bought food, and provided for the children of people who never supported me.

You must decide how much you allow this to affect you. Don't make them right about you by giving up on your dream...

TIME TO SLAY THE

SLAYER...

What is it that you want to get done?

____

____

____

____

____

____

What are you allowing to stop you?

____

____

____

____

____

____

Why is that thing more important that what you want to get done?

____

____

____

____

____

If you put your thing first, how much different would things be for you?

____

____

____

____

____

Is this thing really an issue or you are simply making excuses to get people to stop asking you about it?

____

____

____

____

What's the plan to stop this Slayer from gaining any further ground?

NOW, WHAT DO I DO?

I'm glad that you asked!

Start with ONE of these to work through. You're NOT good where you are if you're looking back at your life and seeing where you have allowed these Slayers to infiltrate your life...

You're NOT good where you are if you can think of something that is no longer available to you and you're upset about it while frantically waiting to see if it comes back to you...

I want you to be HONEST with yourself because they are them and you are you. You are the one who must give an account for what you gave up or allowed to affect you. You can't blame anyone else for what you allowed to affect you or make you give up!

So, I want to issue you a challenge... Take these final pages, choose a Justified Slayer, plan as to how you are going to overcome it, get an accountability partner, share your plan with them, and get over it!

I WILL SLAY THIS SLAYER!

Which Slayer are you going to work on and why?

____

____

____

____

____

What is your plan for overcoming it?

____

____

____

____

____

Who are you going to get to help you stick to your plan?

____

____

____

____

____

How have they said that they will help you?

____

____

____

____

____

What is the plan moving forward?

____

____

____

____

____

How will you measure your progress?

How will you celebrate overcoming this Slayer?

OTHER BOOKS THAT CAN HELP

I want to give you a list of a few more of my books that will help you to do battle with these Justified Slayers. Not only will I list them, but I will also tell you HOW they can help:

- The Real Business Women Slay Slayers SuperBook series—this 7 book series breaks down each Slayer from the original Slayers book and shows how having ONE active Slayer can affect a myriad of areas of your life and business.

- Warrior Women: Overcoming the Slayers God's Way—this book takes the original Slayers and shows how to deal with them Biblically (it will help with some of these, too).

- Every Woman Is A Business Woman: A 30-Day Boot Camp for the Real Business Woman—this will help you plan to not let any Slayer stop you. Your who, what, when, where, why, how, and how much MATTERS! And, there are planners to support you!

- Rise Reclaim Evolve NOW—this workbook breaks down my former business mantra of rising above your frustrations, reclaiming your life and talents, evolving those talents into a treasure, and doing it NOW!
- 12 Rules of Being Dynamically Different—this workbook helps with setting 12 key life and business boundaries and sticking to them.

There are more, but these are the most pertinent ones! You can find them on the following websites: Amazon, Barnes and Noble, BooksAMillion, and Novel Memphis. Alternatively, you can visit my website at http://tammieterrellmompreneurs.com/bookstore and ordering autographed copies!

www.ingramcontent.com/pod-product-compliance
Lightning Source LLC
Chambersburg PA
CBHW020646160726
47991CB00003B/1051